Titles by Markeia Deloney

Level Up After Divorce: A Woman's Guide to Turning Heartache into Happiness

Love Life on Trial: Dating Rehab and Detox for Women

Love Life on Trial:

Dating Rehab and Detox for Women

Love Life on Trial:

Dating Rehab and Detox for Women

MARKEIA DELONEY

Published by Mo Publishing LLC

Quality People Only Please: Tips and Secrets for Women While Dating

ISBN: 978-1-64660-017-5

Dedications

-I dedicate this book to women who want to develop romantic relationships that lead to marriage.

Acknowledgements

Thank you, my parents Mark and Antoinette Lassien, for being my first example of what it means to love and be loved. Your commitment to love each other was a form of loving me. Thank you, my husband Richard Deloney for never being afraid to express your love to me. Your love for me is undeniable. Thank you, my children for teaching me how to love unconditionally. Thank you, my sisters and brothers for being my friends and my loving support system. I love and appreciate you all. Last but not least, the one who first loved me. I thank my Lord and Savior Jesus Christ. Greater love hath no man than this, that a man would lay down his life for his friends (John 15:13NKJ).

CONTENTS

Introduction

Today your love life is under investigation. Dating and having no luck with men can be discouraging, but don't panic. Admitting your mistakes in dating isn't a weakness. The road to love and marriage is a journey, and you are bound to make some wrong turns along the way. When you're dating, it's vital to quickly weed out those individuals who are not ideal for you so that you can develop connections with the right people. This book gives you the keys to recognize relationships that add value to your life. In a world where we watch our society discourage monogamy, committed relationships, exclusivity amongst partners, and marriage altogether, I applaud you for upholding God's standard. I pray that you seek out relationships that will evolve into covenant marriages that are instituted by God's design. I pray that you build healthy, loving families that will serve as the foundation of our communities and continue to influence our society for generations to come.

Part One

The Trial

Bailiff: Order in the court! Court is now in session. The honorable judge presiding on the matter of being a woman while dating.

Judge: Everyone except the people reading this book you all may be seated. Bailiff please swear in the readers of this book

Bailiff: Readers please raise your right hand. Do you solemnly swear or affirm that you will truly listen to this case and render a true verdict and a fair sentence as to this defendant? (readers should answer "I Do"). You may be seated.

Judge: Readers of the book, your duty today will be to determine whether the defense is guilty or not guilty based on the evidence provided in this book. The prosecution has the burden of proving the guilt of the defendant beyond a reasonable doubt. This burden remains on the readers of this book through the trial. The prosecution must prove that the crime was committed, and that the defendant is the person who committed the crime.

Bailiff: Your honor, today's case is Women versus The Dating Scene.

Judge: Is the prosecution ready?

Prosecution: Yes, Your Honor.

Judge: Is the defense ready?

Defense: Yes, Your Honor.

Judge: Prosecution you may call your first witness to the stand

Prosecution: Thank you your honor, we are representing the Dating Scene and we intend to prove that the defendant is guilty of Dating While Being a Woman in the first degree. Your honor, I have several witnesses, but I would first like to call to the stand,

Mr Popcorn Head.

Listen to the description of several witnesses that you may or may not recognize as they take the stand.

Mr. Popcorn Head

Women, is it true that you recognize Mr. Popcorn head?

His description: He was a guy you dated, and the two of you exchanged numbers. He asked you on a date or two, but nothing significant ever came of the encounters. Several months passed, and you did not hear from him.

But on the night in question, you grabbed your phone, and to your surprise, there, his name was popping up across your screen. He texted you; he slid into your DMs, or he has hit your line asking you the age-old infamous question, "what are you doing tonight?" In that moment did you think to yourself, ('I am minding my business, sir")! ("I haven't heard from you in months"). ("Why are you suddenly concerned about what I am doing")?

Could it be that this man thinks he has the luxury of popping up in your life every now and then to waste your time just to let you know he's still around? Hence the name popcorn head, popping up like popcorn! Is it true that you fully knew the facts about this man, yet you willingly still got up, got dressed, and went out to see him when he called you out of the blue?

Mr. Sugar Daddy

Women, is it true that you recognize Mr. Sugar Daddy?

His description: On the day in question, were you walking through the mall at approximately 2:00 PM? Is it true that around about that time you heard a voice say, ("girl you must be tired because you've been running through my mind all day")!

Is it true that at that time you smelled the scent of Old Spice Cologne? Did you turn around and see this man, Mr. Sugar Daddy, old enough to be your grandpa, standing there trying to get your attention? Is it fair to say that you immediately knew that he was an old player from the Himalayas? Did Mr. Sugar Daddy want to spend some money on you and have some fun?

Is it true that you liked the idea of shopping and him fronting the bill? Come on; you knew that this guy was just weeks away from becoming a resident at the Shady Pine Retirement Home. What did you think grandpa was expecting in return from you after showering you with gifts? The thought of it is cringe-worthy, right? Is it true that you smiled at this guy and kept walking, or did you take his gifts?

Mr. Ghost

Women, is it true that you recognize Mr. Ghost?

His description: He was a man you met that seemed rather nice. The two of you hit it off. He soon asked you if you would like to link up and go out with him. You saw no harm in that, so you agreed to go out with him.

On the night in question, is it true that he took you to a club? Did you ask yourself ("why doesn't he want to go to a restaurant")? ("Why not somewhere quiet where we can talk")?

Because Mr. Ghost wasn't interested in getting to know you. Hedidn't like to be alone one-on-one with you unless he was trying to get physical with you, and you know what I mean by getting physical, okay!

The reason Mr. Ghost loved taking you to noisy heavily populated places like the club was to avoid having a meaningful conversation with you. Mr. Ghost never wanted to take you anywhere that would put him into a position where you'd have each other's undivided attention. He didn't want to have to deal with answering all your questions as you attempted to get to know him on a personal level.

Could it be that this man knew he was going to make a clean break from you all along? Is it true that as soon as he got what he wanted from you, you did not see him or hear from him again? Hence the name Ghost. Is it true that you still think about him, and would answer an unexpected phone call from him? Is it true that you would go out with him again if he happened to reappear?

Mr. Blast From The Past

Women, is it true that you recognize Mr. Blast From The Past?

His description: The dating process gets lonely sometimes. Of this, I am aware. Is it accurate to say that you had a guy from your past resurface in your life? Somehow, he caught wind that you were single. He was a guy you knew from way back when.

He had a crush on you in high school, but a romantic relationship never evolved. Is it true that it felt safe and familiar when you were with him? Is that why the two of you spent so much time together? Is itaccurate to say that the two of you reminisced, laughed, and talked for hours?

But in the time you spent with him, you could not deny that not much about him had changed over the years. He was a fool back then, and now he's just an older fool. You couldn't take him seriously as dating material, but you knew that if you called him, he would always show up! No matter what time of night, he'd be ready and available. This guy took you about as seriously as you took him. He had no intention of developing a committed relationship.

The both of you were only filling a need. Being fully aware of the facts concerning this man, is it true that you willfully continued to call Mr. Blast From The Past whenever you felt lonely?

Mr. Married Guy

Women, is it true that you recognize Mr. Married Guy?

His description: He was this fantastic guy you met. He was handsome and charming. He said all the right things. He took you on the most romantic dates. It seemed like he knew exactly how to make you feel special. Well, he did know how to sweep a woman off her feet. You know why? Because his wife had trained him very well. He's had a lot of practice wining and dining her. Therefore, he appeared to be the perfect gentleman to you.

Come down out of the clouds pining over him and think about the facts. Is it accurate to say that all the great moments that the two of you shared only took place early in the day? Is it true that he only took you out to lunch and never dinner? Hello! Why did his phone calls and texts stop abruptly in the evening?

Could it be that it's because he was at home with his wife, and probably a couple of adorable kids, and a puppy too? Having all the facts concerning Mr. Married Guy, did you continue to close your eyes to the clues suggesting that he may be married? Is it true that you continued to date him without confirming his martial status?

Mr. Mess Around

Women, is it true that you recognize Mr. Mess Around?

His Description: You met this guy, you thought he was alright, but you made no advances. You played it cool. You even had your eye on another guy in the room anyway. But this guy was zoned in on you. He pursued you, even when you showed minimal interest, he continued to chase you harder and harder.

He acted as though he had to have you, and his consistent attempt to get your attention made you feel flattered. Eventually, you spent some time with him, and you enjoyed yourself.

On the day in question, some time had passed since you'd met Mr. Mess Around. Is it true that you were walking and saw Mr. Mess around headed in your direction? You called his name and waved at him. But to your surprise, he was walking towards the lady a few steps ahead of you. At that time did old Mess Around pretend that you didn't even exist?

You appeared to be a crazy person waving and yelling because you waved at him and yelled out, (Hey Brian!") when his name was actually Brad. He lied to you about everything! Could it be that he was a professional cheater? Cheating was his forte, this wasn't his first time, and it wouldn't be his last. After having all the facts concerning Mr. Mess Around, is it true that you still called him and received phone calls from him? Is it true that you even met up with him after knowing he was sleeping around with everyone?

Mr. Poet

Women, is it true that you recognize Mr. Poet?

His description: You worked with this guy. He was the one who overheard about your last bad breakup, and he jumped at the opportunity to catch you on the rebound. He came to your side and whispered in your ear and said sweet things like, "how are you holding up beautiful, you know love can and does die, but true love is forever." How about you let me be your forever?" You could literally melt as he spoke. But while you were getting googly-eyed, he was googling more love quotes to say to you. He knew what he wanted from you, and he knew how to get it. The guy was defiantly not that profound.

Is it safe to say that you fell for his sweet words at a time when you were most vulnerable? Could it be that you were still sad about your last lousy breakup and turned to Mr. Poet for comfort? Mr. Poet knew you were weak. He knew that he could tell you the most romantic things and make all sorts of promises to you without the burden of having ever to prove them. After knowing these facts about Mr. Poet, did you continue to be an easy target for him? Did you continue to jump from relationship to relationship without giving yourself time to heal from the previous one?

Mr. Mommas Boy

Women, is it true that you recognize Mr. Mommas Boy?

His description: You met this guy; he was an excellent man. He was always available to talk on the phone when you called. But on the night in question when you were ready to go out with him for a romantic evening, is it true that he said that he couldn't make it because he had to take his mother to her choir rehearsal practice? Is it safe to say that he always seemed to have to cancel the plans the two of you made to go help his mom with something? Your quality time together was always interrupted.

He would have to jump up and go mow his moms' yard. He would have to cut the night short with you to go drive his mom and her girlfriends to senior night at the bingo hall.

We all love our moms don't get me wrong, but when you see this pattern being a reoccurring situation, you start to think that the guy is attached to his mother at the hip in an unhealthy way. Is it true that you continued to date him as he tried to juggle his time between you and his mom? Is it true that you were pushed to the back burner and always took second place to his obligations to his mother? Is it safe to say you knew you needed more attention in a relationship, but you continued to date Mr. Mommas Boy?

Mr. Fixer Upper

Women, is it true that you recognize Mr. Fixer Upper?

His description: You met a guy, and he was a little rough around the edges. Okay, who am I kidding? He was extremely rough around the front, the back, the top, the bottom, the left, and the right, not just the edges. As women, we tend to date potential. Is it safe to say that you were only looking at what the man could be while ignoring what he was? Is it accurate to say that you took him on as your personal project?

Did you see the red flags slapping you right in the face, but you ignored the warnings thinking you'd be the one to fix the man up? Taking on a fixer-upper could work if you have the time and energy. However, the real transformation of any individual only takes place if that person is ready to make a change? The man may have been nice, but he was not your project. Is it true that you knew Mr. Fixer Upper wasn't willing to change, but you kept telling yourself that you'd be the one to change him?

Mr. Friendzone

Women, is it true that you recognize Mr. Friendzone?

His description: He was totally into you, but you didn't find him physically attractive. Would it be correct to say that you enjoyed his company and liked his personality? You knew the guy was falling for you. He always called you. He always asked you out to dinner, you were always hungry, so you would go and have a good time. Is it safe to say that you'd be doing both of you a favor by making the next restaurant visit with this guy you're last?

I know the food is fantastic at that restaurant. I get that. Okay, you can take a doggy bag, but you know good and well that you would never fall in love with this guy. Is it true that you only saw him as a friend? Is it true that you continued to go out with Mr. Friendzone whenever he asked? Is it true that you were toying with the emotions of a man who was falling in love with you? Were you aware that leading a man on could be dangerous?

Perhaps, plenty of other women out there would find this man attractive, yet you stood in the way by not allowing him to expend his time and energy in their direction! Is it true that if you were always on dates with Mr. Friendzone, you were limiting your chances of meeting a guy you were really attracted to?

Mr. Workaholic

Women, is it true that you recognize Mr. Workaholic?

His description: You were communicating with him, and you realized that he spent a lot of time at work. Is it true that every single time you were out on a date with this guy, his overactive cellphone accompanied the two of you? On the night in question, is it safe to say that he was continually receiving calls, checking, emails, and paying very little attention to you or anything you had to say? The guy wasn't bad. Would it be accurate to say that he was in a phase of his life where he couldn't find the right balance between work and relationships?

Is it safe to say that you love a guy who's driven and motivated to succeed in his career? We, as women, take pride in our careers as well. But is it true that you would prefer to date a guy who valued the time he shared with you? Is it true that you would like a guy to be able to ignore a few calls while the two of you were together? Knowing all the facts as it relates to Mr. Workaholic, did you continue to date him?

Mr. Penny Pincher

Women, is it true that you recognize Mr. Penny Pincher?

His description: The first time you went out with this guy, you adored the romantic picnic in the park he set up for the two of you. The next date, he wanted to take you for a walk around the trail in your neighborhood, and you enjoyed that date too. On the night in question, did you decide to go out to a romantic dinner at a great restaurant with Mr. Penny Pincher? When you got to the restaurant, you wanted to order wine. But is it true that old Penny Pincher ordered water with lemon for the both of you? Did he reach for the sugar packets on the table? Did he begin to add enough sugar packets to the lemon water to make lemonade?

Is it correct to say that you were embarrassed! Is it true that you were hungry and looking forward to ordering a juicy steak and some mashed potatoes? However, before you could open your mouth to tell the waiter what you wanted, your guy ordered an appetizer for the two of you to share.

When the waiter came by and asked if you were interested in dessert, before you could answer your cheap date, insisted that the two of you were stuffed and couldn't possibly eat another bite. You finally realized that all the dates the guy had taken you on before this one was totally free. The dates didn't cost him a dime. Is it fair to say that the guy was a cheapskate? Did you really want to have to pinch pennies when you were out on the town with your man? I think not. After the lemon water and appetizers, you were still hungry. After having all the facts, did you continue to date, Mr. Penny Pincher?

Mr. Gamer

Women, is it true that you recognize Mr. Gamer?

His description: You had been dating this guy for some time; he seemed fine. On the day in question, you were spending the day at his place. You were sitting on the couch watching TV, and you dozed off. Would it be accurate to say that you woke up startled by extremely loud voices yelling ("boy you trash")! Is it true that you looked up and saw your guy sitting two inches away from his flatscreen, wearing a headset, with an Xbox controller in his hands talking to people he didn't know online, yelling, and screaming at his game? He did not even realize that you had woken up for several minutes.

So, then you patiently waited for him to finish his game. But is it true that five minutes of waiting turned into fifteen, fifteen minutes turned into thirty, and the next thing you knew an hour had gone by and he still hadn't stopped playing the game? Is it true that you sweetly asked him to hurry up and finish the game, and he immediately turned and yelled, ("Can't you see I'm in the middle of a game!") You quickly realized that the guy spent way too much time on his game. An occasional time playing 2K and Madden was fine, but every day like clockwork, no sir, I will pass.

After seeing Mr. Gamer's unwillingness to focus on you, did you continue to date him?

Mr. Social Media

Women, is it true that you recognize Mr. Social Media?

His description: This guy looked nice, so the two of you started dating regularly. You noticed that he posted a lot on social media. We all love adding our pictures and highlighting unforgettable moments on the gram, but some people are just extreme with it. You saw that this guy posted from sunup to sundown. His posts throughout one day went a little something like this. ("Hey everyone, I just brushed my teeth!)" Picture of him with his toothbrush. ("Hi, people I'm back after a hard workout, hopping in the shower.)" There's his picture flexing in a towel! Then, of course, there's a picture of him with a plate of his avocado toast he's having for breakfast. And he continued like this all day every day.

Is it fair to say that he would do anything for a photo? Is it true that he would do anything for clout? Is it correct that he was not a social influencer? Therefore, was not making any money from posting his pictures. Talk about attention-seeking. It's just too much. Is it true that you wanted to leave him to his flexing and filters? Did you want to leave him to the validation of invisible people hearting his photos? After having all the facts as it relates to Mr. Social Media, did you continue to date him?

Mr. Opportunist

Women, is it true that you recognize Mr. Opportunist?

His description: He sees you as an opportunity rather than a serious relationship. He is the guy you can find sleeping on his couch in the middle of the day. You met this man, and right away, you realized he wasn't on your level financially. But you gave him a chance anyway because you are not a shallow person. You believed in his ability to grow and change. But you quickly learned after your second, or third date that the guy always forgot his wallet at home, and he couldn't even afford to buy you a cheap burger.

Is it fair to say that you were patient with him to see if he had any intentions of moving beyond his current financial situation? Is it true the guy showed you with his actions, that he had no ambition, or any desire to change? This guy was going nowhere and getting there fast! He was hoping he could get there on your coat tail. Did you want to pick up an extra burden, and disguise him as your man? Knowing all the facts as it pertains to Mr. Opportunist, did you continue to date him?

Mr. It's Complicated

Women, is it true that you recognize Mr. It's Complicated?

His description: You met this guy, and he was charming. You were feeling his vibe. The two of you went out on several occasions, and everything seemed to be going smoothly. On the night in question, is it true that you were hanging out with him, and you overheard him arguing with someone on his phone? You were able to make out that it was a woman's voice on the line. Is it accurate to say that you didn't want to intrude, so you didn't push the issue? When Mr. It's Complicated finished his conversation, he came back in and said that he was on the phone with his child's mother and that she was letting him know that his daughter was sick. He told you that he needed to go and meet them at the ER.

You said sure, and then he ran out the door. When the two of you met up again, you noticed that he was getting lots of alerts and phone calls. You recognized that it was the same woman's voice back on the phone as the previous night. You finally asked him what was going on. And he said, "it's complicated!" He sat you down and said there was something he had to tell you. At that time, you learned that the woman calling was his wife, and the two of them were separated but still lived together.

He told you not to worry about it because he did not love her and was going to divorce her. Is it true that Mr. It's complicated should have told you he was legally married when you first met? Is it accurate to say that you never saw court-ordered documents that verified his divorce was in process? Perhaps you should have said, "No, sir, call me when you finalize your divorce!" Having all the facts concerning this man did you still continue to date him?

Mr. Catfish

Women, is it true that you recognize Mr. Catfish?

His description: You met this guy online. You saw his request in your inbox. You accepted the request. When you scrolled through his profile, you were excited about what you saw. Is it accurate to say that you thought Mr. Catfish was handsome and physically fit, you thought to yourself, he must be athletic? You were blown away when you came across a picture of him skydiving, you thought to yourself; he must be adventurous. You saw intellectual quotes he had posted. You thought to yourself, he must be intelligent. To top it off, he wore a suit coat in a lot of his pictures. Yes! That's a winner he was gainfully employed and successful.

The two of you began to communicate. Is it true that you would wake up to a "good morning beautiful" text message from him every day? The two of you would text back and forth all day long. When you got home from work you would call him and talk until you fell asleep. After some time went by, you were interested in meeting up with him. But every time the two of you tried to meet up, Mr. Catfish would have an outlandish story about why he wasn't going to be able to make it. If it wasn't his car tires blowing out on the highway, then it was his apartment being robbed.

You were anxious to meet him. Finally, the day came where the two of you were going to meet up. On the day in question, you were having one of those amazing days where your hair was laying just right. Your skin was glowing; makeup was flawless. You slipped into your black dress and were ready to go. You drove down the highway, super excited, ready to have fun. You arrived at the restaurant before your date. He sent you a message saying he was pulling up outside. So, you took your seat, had a big smile on your face patiently waiting.

In came this guy walking up to your table, his arm extended, reaching out to shake your hand. He said, "nice to finally meet you and told you that you looked beautiful." Too bad, you couldn't say the same. The guy looked nothing like his pictures. Well, he did have a suit coat on, but his beer belly was lapped so far over his pants you hardly noticed. Is it true that the pictures on his profile must have been from at least ten years ago? Would it be accurate to say that you were disappointed that your date wasn't who he said he was? Having all the facts, did you continue to spend too much time and energy entertaining men on social media who you were not certain were who they said they were?

Mr. Pie in the Sky

Women, is it true that you recognize Mr. Pie in the Sky?

His description: This man may be considered the most dangerous of them all. You got involved with this guy, and he turned out to be more like a "situationship" than a relationship You were really into him. The physical attraction and chemistry were undeniable. The two of you got close and were together for three years. You even relocated to be closer to him in hopes of the relationship, eventually growing into marriage. This guy promised you the world, but he still owed the world to the last girl, he made that empty promise too. He told you he wanted to marry you one day and take care of you. He told you he wanted to start a family withyou. The two of you even picked out names for your future children.

He said he'd be the sole provider for your family, and you wouldn't have to lift a finger. Before you knew it, you looked up, and you had spent another year waiting on all of his promises. On the night in question, is it true that the two of you went out for dinner to celebrate another year of your relationship? Would it be accurate to say that you were expecting a ring from your guy that evening?

As much as he talked about marrying you, were you convinced that you were going to walk out of that restaurant engaged? But nope, there was no proposal; there was nothing! Perhaps, this guy was only selling you a false dream? Hence the name Pie in the Sky. From what you've witnessed after spending years with this man, is it safe to say that he does not intend to make you his wife? Could it be that the guy was most definitely enjoying reaping the benefits of having you do all the things a wife would do just minus the commitment and the marriage?

You've heard the old adage, "why buy the cow when you can get the milk for free?" Is it true that he always had an excuse when you asked him about marriage? His favorite was, "well, you know, baby, I just want to give you the wedding of your dreams, and I need to get my finances in order first." Honestly, at this point you would have been happy marrying the guy at a simple ceremony wearing a burlap sack. Knowing full well that Mr. Pie in the Sky had no interest in making you his wife, is it true that you continued to play house with him?

Prosecution: The prosecution rests, no further questions your Honor.

Judge: Mr. Pie in the Sky you may step down.

Judge: Defense you may call your first witness to the stand?

Defense: Thank you your Honor. Today we only have one witness. The Defense would like to call Mr. Keeper to the stand.

Mr. Keeper

Women, is it true that you recognize Mr. Keeper?

His description : Is it accurate to say that this is the guy we all want? He is attractive, educated, responsible, and well-spoken. He is a financially secure man. That's code for he has a job. You're free to be yourself when you're with him. He compliments you and your personality. You have the same core values that will lead you to a common ground during stressful situations. He respects you. He is open and honest with you. He shows you his love through the sacrifices he is willing to make for you. Any guy who is worth your while must know how to treat you like the queen that you are. He protects you.

Any guy who will cover you and have your back is a quality guy. He will profess his love for you. Any guy who is genuinely interested in you on an exclusive level will want to mark his territory. He will want to make it clear to others that you are his lady, no doubt about it. He will slap a title on you so quickly because he sees your value. He won't hesitate to allow you to meet his family and the people who are most important in his life. When he introduces you to everyone, it will be as his woman. At no time will he say, "Hey, everyone, I'd like you to meet my friend." He doesn't have that luxury. He knows that you're an amazing woman, and if he doesn't claim you eventually, some other man will snatch you up. The wrong guy can have his eyes peeled back and fastened to his forehead with safety pins looking you dead in your face and won't be able to recognize your value, and that's fine let him walk. Mr. keeper will know your value from a mile away. Wait on him.

Defense: The defense rests its case; no further questions your Honor.

Part Two

The Deliberation

Readers it is now time to deliberate.

Judge: Readers of this book, you have heard all of the testimony concerning the case of Women versus The Dating Scene. It is now up to you to determine the facts. You and you alone are the judges of the facts. Once you decide what facts the evidence proves, you must then apply the law as I give it to you to the facts as you find them.

The LAW

> Law of Love Statue Women's Intuition DATING IN THE FIRST DEGREE: Failure to consider the warnings and follow your heart. Whoever intentionally welcomes unfavorable circumstances that cause damage to one's self-esteem, physical/emotional well-being, and productivity may be sentenced to the Dating Rehab and Detox program of this book. They may not be released to date until they complete the 6-step program.

Judge: Readers have you reached a verdict?

Readers of this book: should say (We have, your Honor).

Judge: What say you?

Readers: Readers should say (We the readers, in the case of Women versus The Dating Scene, find the defendant guilty of the charge of DATING IN THE FIRST DEGREE.)

Judge: Thank you, readers, for your service today. You must complete the 6-Step Dating Rehab and Detox for Women Program in this book. Court is adjourned!

Part Three

Dating Rehab and Detox

Dating Rehab and Detox 6 step Action Program for Women

Step 1

Date yourself

Requirement

It is important to be comfortable enjoying your own company. You should know what you like doing and be able to share those things with a man. If you can't enjoy being alone with you, what makes you think that others will? What is your favorite restaurant? Do you prefer soul food, Mexican food, or Italian food?

Do you like action, comedy, drama, or horror moves? What are your hobbies? Please know what you like! Take yourself to the movies. Take yourself out to dinner. Go enjoy one of your favorite activities.You are required to take yourself out this weekend!

Benefit

The benefit of dating yourself is that you will learn to be content. You won't be consumed with finding a man. You will be having a blast in your singleness. Plase don't confuse being single with being whole. You can be completely whole while you are single. You won't be seeking a person to complete you because you are already complete.

The man coming into your life will only add value, not create it. You are valuable all by yourself.And when you find yourself a joy to be around, then men will too. You must love yourself first, before you can truly love someone else.

Sign/date each action step as you complete

Step 2

Know your values and honor what you want

Requirement

There are core values that we all have. Those values should be unshakable. For example. Do you value family, marriage, having a relationship with God, education etc. Know and list your values. Because they are the foundation of who you are and who you will become.

Please remember that you can never receive what you do not honor/respect. For example, if you talk negatively about everyone who is married, and hate seeing happy couples post their pictures on social media, and you say things like, that's just for show I know they are having problems, and so forth then love and marriage will avoid you!(everyone has problems in marriage, but two willing partners can always improve their relationship whenever they choose) But you just sprayed yourself with man repellent when you think and speak that way about others! You must celebrate and honor the thngs you desire to see manifest in your own life. If not, you are sending out signals that say you have no interest in marriage, which is a lie. Because most of the time the people who speak so negatively and show the most irritation about other's love and marriage, are the people who desire it the most. But because of the way you dishonor anyone attempting to be happily married is the reason you can't have a loving relationship enter your life.

Please watch your words and stop speaking from a place of disappointment when it comes to love and marriage and speak from a place of hope. That is how you say you are ready and welcome love into your life. First, You are required to do a full self investigation on your attitude and words towards love and marriage. Second, you are required to get a pen and paper and write down your core values. Please remember that admitting our mistakes isn't weakness, it is growth.

Benefit

The benefit of knowing your values is that you can select men who are better suited to date you. You and your partner will not struggle to agree on, and make decisions about major issues such as marriage, monogamy, parenting, work ethic, religion, and other life- altering factors as a result. Choosing individuals with shared values will reduce stress in your relationship. When you know this, you won't select partners who require you to convince them to see your perspective. You won't feel pressured to change your beliefs to be with them. You can comfortably be 100% your authentic self. We all want a partner that allows us to be ourselves.

You also get to take the guess work out of dating. If you intend to be married simply ask a man if marriage is a core value of his. I promise you that a man that's not interested in marriage will let you know. You just have to pay attention to his words. If he says things like, I'm just having fun, I'm just taking it one day at a time, or Let's just go with the flow. Nine times out of ten he is not interested in commitment and marriage. Listen to hear if he says things like, I am a family man. I am ready for a serious relationship. I consider myself to be a one- woman-man, playing the field dosent interest me anymore. Seriously, just pay attention and outright ask him the question to avoid dating someone who isn't seeking what you are seeking. That is the number one question you need to have answered before you give your time and attention to a man.

You will take the complication out of choosing a partner by selecting people who are already on the same page, which means they share the same values.

Sign/date each action step as you complete

Step 3

Know who you are and what you bring to the table.

Be an asset not a liability.

Requirement

When a man gets you, what is he getting? It is essential to know the value that you bring to a man's life. For example, would you make him laugh? Would you be a good listener? What skill do you have to increase his wellbeing overall? Can you whip up a fabulous meal? Are you a great money manager? What makes you special? What makes you great? What are the things that you are good at? What are the things that you are confident that if need be, you could do them in your sleep?

A common mistake woman make is to think a great guy is going to come and rescue them. But nobody wants to take on a burden, they want someone who can help lighten the load. A man dosnt wake up in the morning and say to himself, "I can't wait to meet a woman so I can pay all her bills and student loans!"

You are required to get a pen and paper and answer these questions.

Question 1- What is a man getting when he gets me?

Question 2- How can I increase a man's happiness, his health, and his wealth?

Benefit

The benefit in knowing who you are and what you bring to the table is that you will be full of self-respect. You will be confident about who you are and the value that you can add to a man's life. Some may even call you arrogant, and that's perfectly fine!

You won't need a man to complete or validate you. At best, he can only add to who you already are. You will know that you are a blessing to a man.

You will know that it is an honor and a privilege for anyone lucky enough to have you in their life. Because you know that their life is going to improve on every level because you showed up. That's just how amazing of a waman you are!You won't compete with or compare yourself to anyone. You won't be intimidated by anyone. You won't waste your time with people who don't appreciate what you bring. You will understand that if a man can't see your value, it's their loss, and they lack the capacity to receive all your brilliance. You will be able to ignore them and choose partners that enhance your life as you do the same for them in return.

Sign/date each action step as you complete

Step 4

Have a life

Requirement

Be sure that you are living your life to the fullest. Have goals for yourself that you are actively working on. Feel good in your skin. Join a workout group. Keep your hair and nails done. wear beautiful outfits and go strut your stuff. Contribute to humanity by getting involved with local groups, and programs that are making a difference in your community. Have friends. Have hobbies. Have interests. Your life needs to be productive and full of activities, events, trips, etc. that you are looking forward too.

You are required to go out and buy a calendar. Find events to attend. Find a workout class to commit to. Schedule time to hang out with friends and family. Plan a vacation and start saving for the trip.Find a fabulous hairstylist make an appointment and get an updated look, Take up a new hobby. Etc. the point is to find things to do and write them on your calendar. Find things that you are interested in and things that push you past your comfort zone.

Benefit

The benefit in having a full life is that men are attracted to women who are independent and managing their lives well. Men like women who are exciting and interesting. (You can't be interesting if you have no interests) You should be so full of life and joy that when a man looks at you, he says I want to go where she's going! I want to do what she's doing! You don't want to be a lame drag who has nothing going on but the same boring routine each day. You got to mix it up! If you are always free when a man calls. He will immediately think that you don't have a life. You will appear desperate, and that's the quickest way to run a quality man off. He will see you as being too needy and possibly a burden.

Sign/date each action step as you complete

Step 5

Know your Standards, Boundaries,and Deal Breakers.

Requirement

Create an application: Please know what you are looking for in a man. Beyond his physical appearance, what is important to you as it relates to your existing goals and ambitions? For example, are you looking to buy a house? Then you would want to consider his credit. Do you already have kids, or want to have kids soon? If so, you will want to find out if he has kids or wants to have kids. Has he had a vasectomy? Please don't make any assumptions.

You must ask questions that matter as it relates to what you want for your life! Consider a man who naturally fits cohesively with your mission, your purpose, and your goals. You must know what you want and where you're going to understand how an additional person would fit into that picture. Know your standards when it comes to men. There should be a set bar to determine if a man is even worth your time. That may sound rude, but it is necessary to avoid people who are not willing to do what it takes to connect with you on a romantic level.

Having standards means knowing the things that you will and will not tolerate from a man. People will only treat you how you allow them to treat you. You have got to train people how to treat you. The way people learn how to treat you is by observing how you treat yourself. Having standards will quickly teach a man that you respect yourself and he must respect you as well, if he doesn't rise to your standard then he dosent value being with you. But by no means will you lower your standard to meet him, he will happily rise to the standard or be removed from your life to make space for the men who are willing to uphold your standard. A man will understand that you are a woman who says what she means, and means what she says. You are grown and did not come to play. You don't have time.

You should have certain things that are deal- breakers for you when it comes to dating to avoid physical, verbal, mental, and emotional abuse. An example of a possible deal- breaker is Violence. If a man physically assaults you then you are DONE, PERIOD!

Whatever your standards and deal-breakers are, have them established before you enter a relationship along with the actions you will take if violated which are your boundaries. Your boundaries say here are the consequences for adverse actions. If a person knows they can treat you any kind of way and get away with it, they will continue to do so. Forget crying and asking a man to explain WHY he did it. I learned long ago that the answer to WHY is simple. It's because he wanted to. He made a bad decision. You don't need to talk about it, you don't need "closure." Close the door in his face there's your closure! The only thing you need to concern yourself with is making new adjustments and arrangements.

Benefit

Benefit is that you will be interested in Quality, not Quantity. You will remain respectable and reduce your headcount. When dating, you don't want to be that woman who is in love with a new man every month. You will immediately know who you should engage with and who you should avoid. Every company has its mission statement, rules, and regulations. And if we apply to work at that business, we must first submit our resume and the employer must determine that we are a good fit for the job.

There is nothing wrong with using the same mindset when it comes to choosing men to date. Aren't you the CEO of the business that is called YOU! Take applications and resumes before you qualify a man. It is okay to take your time selecting a partner.

Sign/date each action step as you complete

Steps 6

Be fully functional

Requirement

Be fully functional before you ever get in a romantic relationship. Make sure that you are managing your life well. Take care of the whole person that is you. consider Your spirituality, education, business, relationships with family and friends, physical and emotional health. Make sure you're a great money manager. you can Be able to pay your own bills on time. Be able to buy anything you want.

Be able to go anywhere you want when you want. Be able to meet your needs on your own. Have your own place to live. Have your own vehicle. Be a great mother if you have kids.

Benefit

The benefit of being fully functional is that you will never have to choose a man out of necessity. You won't rush into marriage for financial security. You won't rush to get married just because all your friends are. You can patiently wait on who God has for you without fearing that you are missing out. Another great benefit about being fully functional is that it helps you avoid abuses of all kinds. You won't have to tolerate men who disrespect you in any way, shape, or form. You call the shots!

Sign/date each action step as you complete

Statistics show that in the US, 50% of first marriages, 67% of second marriages, and 74% of third marriages end in divorce. I discussed the topic with humor, but please understand that you are dating to marry so, choosing the right man is detrimental. It is one of the biggest decisions you will make in life.

You wouldn't go to a car lot and buy the first car you saw. Likewise, it is crucial to take your time in love and relationships and select your partner with caution. It's not just your life you have to think about, but also the lives of the children that are born as a result. From experience, I know that marrying an unsuitable person will bring you heartaches, abuses, and traumas of all kinds. I encourage you to apply the six steps in this book to help you to be proactive in selecting quality partners who will bring out the best in you because that is the real benefit in relationship at its core.

Out of billions of people on earth, there isn't just one person out there thats your one and only soulmate, but there are soles which are willing to bind themselves together by love and commit to doing the work it takes to sustain a bond that lasts a lifetime. Applying the steps in this book is just the beginning, even relationships with the most compatible partners are going to take work and maintenance. Honestly, Mr. right is really Mr. Willing. He is the man who may not be perfect, but he is not selfish. He is willing to work on his marriage. Two willing people can be successful at love. I trust your judgment and know that you are ready to go out and make great choices when it comes to dating.

www.ingramcontent.com/pod-product-compliance
Lightning Source LLC
Chambersburg PA
CBHW051722050726
47598CB00003B/1004

* 9 7 8 1 6 4 6 6 0 0 1 7 5 *